© 1983 by Mirror Group Newspapers Ltd.
First published in Great Britain in 1983
by Mirror Books Ltd., Athene House,
66/73 Shoe Lane, London EC4P 4AB
for Mirror Group Newspapers Ltd.
Printed and bound in Great Britain by
Spottiswoode Ballantyne Ltd.,
Colchester and London

ISBN 0 85939 389 5

Get to know your fellow passengers
1. Wellington and Boot

The next three pages are for the uninitiated; who are probably better off that way—as we can testify. Being initiated is a nasty operation and we wouldn't want to have to go through it twice.

Health matters aside, you would do well to read on before plunging into the pulp. Then you'll at least be familiar with the characters, if not the plot. You'll be grasping for your sanity before you even get a toehold on that.

A glance to the top of the page reveals our two main characters. The enthroned one, a large hairy Old English Sheepdog (sort of) named Boot, is being propelled by a small scruffy Young English Boy called Wellington. Wellington is named after his own footwear from which he's inseparable. This is because of a natural and powerful adhesive he's created by never changing his socks.

Equally inseparable are the boy and his dog—or the dog and his boy—held together by a bond of mutual affection. They jostle upon life's stage, each convinced he's playing the leading role since each believes he's master. This leads to situations such as the one portrayed on the right. Here Boot has wrested the lead from Wellington who is hanging on to a bit part, or to be quite accurate many bit parts—which are in turn hanging on to him.

One more piece of intelligence may prove useful in a tight corner, and believe us you'll find yourself in several: Boot believes he's not a dog at all but an eighteenth century English Lord condemned to assume the mantle of a quadruped rug by the black arts of a gipsy wench with whom he had some dalliance. Or was it dilliance? Whatever it was it was powerful stuff and back in the eighteenth century they're still picking up the clothespegs.

KISS KISS KISS

2. Maisie and Marlon

Another inseparable pair is Maisie and Marlon. No, wait—that's not quite true. Marlon is fully detached, in more ways than one. It's *Maisie* who does the clinging, when she can, and the clanging, usually on Marlon's head, when she can't.

You can see them performing, top left, in the roles of a woman prepared to give her all—and a boy prepared to give her plenty of room in which to give it.

Marlon hopes to grow into the figure of a fine upstanding man, and hopes too, that somehow someone will supply a brain to go with it.

Maisie hopes to grow to be a woman but everybody else, judging her on appearances and demeanour, expects her to grow into a consignment of surplus army boots—or something equally lumpy. But a woman? Nature can only accomplish so much.

As a career, Marlon can't decide between a Brain Surgeon or a Bloke-Wot-Goes-Down-Sewers-In-Big-Rubber-Boots. Unkind people have pointed out to him the problems of a person without much in the way of brains wanting to be a brain surgeon, but Marlon riposts with "So wot? I also don't 'appen to 'ave any sewers".

Maisie intends to be a "Beautiful an' talented lady pest-exterminator". Only the first part is impossible because a pest-exterminator of formidable power she already is. Her voice has been known to bring every form of undesirable shrieking from the woodwork, begging for the Coup-De-Grace. And that's when she laughs.

3. Baby Grumpling

One pest Maisie has not succeeded in exterminating is her little brother, Baby Grumpling; he of the angelic hair and eyes—a facade designed to camouflage the destructive potential that lurks beneath. Beneath the stairs, beneath the wardrobe, beneath the ground (Grumpling's speciality is digging holes in the flowerbed to converse with the worms)—in all these lairs the Grumpling lurketh, usually with the purpose of ambushing Maisie. Baby Grumpling wants to grow up to be the extremely unpleasant boss of lady pest-exterminators.

It's not that Baby Grumpling has any real animosity towards his sister. It's just that each has a different point of view about a number of things. Things like spiders-in-the-bath (her bath) anties in the panties (her panties) toad-in-the-hole (his toad—her batter) and glue on the loo (a joke which gave Maisie a bit of a fixation).

Grumpling has also achieved fame as a trainer of Olympic worms. His methods are based on paternalism and participation at all levels. Even if an aspiring worm fails to make the grade as an athlete, Grumpling still absorbs it into the organisation. He eats it.

Before Grumpling's advent Maisie had been campaigning for a puppy. Now she is of the opinion that her mother has a truly weird sense of humour.

On your journey through this Omnibus you'll encounter other characters. In the canine category there's a bloodhound of Indian derivation, BH. (Calcutta) Failed. There's Tatty Oldbitt (the sailor's friend) and blundering Beryl Bogey. An echelon of flies will herald the approach of Dirty McSquirty. You will probably also come across a number of pages a-crawl with crabs. Remain calm. No harm will be offered you by any of these characters—provided you remember the passwords "I've paid cash for this here book".

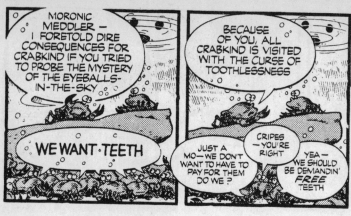

0.227

0.228

O.231

O.232

O.245

Panel 1: HAVIN' ESTABLISHED THAT SATURDAY OCTOBER 25th IS MY BIRTHDAY / WE COME TO THE SUBJECT OF...

Panel 2: PRESENTS

Panel 3: ANY QUESTIONS?

Panel 4: WASN' IT NICE OF MISS DIMMO TO LET US DO WELLIN'TONS BIRTHDAY CARD AS A PAINTIN' PROJECT / YEA — MIND YOU, PROJECTIN' PAINT AIN'T ALL THAT EASY

Panel: HOW D'YOU PAINT A FROG? / WIV GREAT DIFFICULTY

Panel: YOU'VE JUST SMUDGED MY DELICATE TRACERY OF LEAF AN' FERN — RATBAG

Panel: AN' DON'T YOU GO BLABBING TO WELLIN'TON ABOUT THIS, MARLON / DON' YOU WORRY, MAISIE — MY LIPS IS SEALED

O.246

Panel: H'LO, MARLON? / WHERE ARE ALL THE OTHERS? / WHAT'S GOIN' ON ROUN' HERE? / CRUMBS — WHAT A MESS YOU'RE IN

Panel: SORRY, WELLIN'TON — MY LIPS IS SEALED / OTHERWISE IT WON'T BE THE SECRET SURPRISE IT'S STILL GOIN' TO BE ON ACCOUNT OF I DIDN'T SAY A WORD

O.251

O.252

0.255

WELLIN'TON —WHAT *ARE* YOU DOIN' WITH OUR BIRTHDAY CARD?

ER...ER... *WALKIES*, THEN, BIRTHDAY CARD? THERE'S A NICE BIRTHDAY CARD, *WALKIES?*

0.256

HAPPY BRI'DAY WELL'N'TON

♪

HEY, SONNY— YOU DROPPED SOMETHING

O.271

O.272

THIS IS *IT* —THIS BOOK COULD CHANGE MY WHOLE LIFE

"...THE MARVEL OF POS·I·TIVE THIN·KING"

LIBRARY HOURS

RIGHT— EYES DOWN

MMMMM MMMMM MMMMM

MMMMM MMMMM

O.273

MMMMM...

WOT DOES 'POS·I·TIVE' MEAN?

WELLIN'TON— WHY'VE YOU BEEN GOIN' ROUN' CALLIN' MY MARLON A FAILURE?

WELL AS A MATTER O'FAC' MAISIE —I HAVEN'T

MARLON'S BEEN GOIN' ROUN' CALLIN' MARLON A FAILURE

AN' I SUPPOSE YOU *AGREED* WITH HIM

NO—I *DIDN'T*

COULDN' YOU FOR ONCE IN YOUR LIFE BUILD UP MARLON'S *CONFIDENCE* AN' *AGREE* WITH HIM?

O.274

O.275

O.276

0.279

0.280

YOU KNOW — WITH YOU I CAN SPEND HOURS AND HOURS WITHOUT THE NECESSITY TO UTTER A SINGLE WORD

I'M NOT MUCH FOR DALLIANCE BUT 'PON MY SOUL MA'AM — WITH YOU I'VE KNOWN CONTENTMENT

...IT *IS*... MA'AM...ISN'T IT ?

I *REPEAT* MA'AM — YOU *ARE* A MADAM, MISS, MS OR SOMETHING APPROXIMATE ARE YOU NOT ?

DEY-VIL TAKE IT — YOU'VE BEEN THE RECIPIENT OF MY MOST INTIMATE THOUGHTS — STATE YOUR GENDER — I'LL HAVE AN ANSWER IF YOU PLEASE

DAMNATION SIRRAH — ANY MORE OF THIS DUMB INSOLENCE AND I'LL CALL YOU OUT — D'YOU HEAR ?

YOU IDLE SKINNY WRETCH, I'M GOING TO MOP THE FLOOR WITH YOU

0.301

0.302

MARLON — ARE YOU GOIN' TO TELL ME ABOUT MY CHRIS'MAS PREZZY?

I SPOSE YOU *ARE* GOIN' TO *GIVE* ME A CHRIS'MAS PREZZY?

WELL *ALL RIGHT* MAISIE

— IT'S ONE O'THEM HUGE OLE VICTORIAN DOLLS-HOUSES

WHICH I'M MAKIN' MYSELF

ENTIRELY OUT OF USED MATCHSTICKS

— IT *COULD* TAKE A LITTLE TIME

0.303

WELL — IT WASN'T ONE OF THE MOST ELEGANT CHRIS'MAS DINNERS, BOOT, BUT THERE CERTAINLY WAS ENOUGH OF IT

WE'RE STUFFED FULL

OR YOU MIGHT SAY REPLETE

BURP

— SORRY I THOUGHT YOU SAID *REPEAT*

0.304

0.307

P.1

AHA! **AAAGH**

I'M A POOR GIRL— I COME FROM A VERY POOR FAMILY

YES—YES— I KNOW—YOUR FATHER'S POOR YOUR MOTHER'S POOR YOUR MAID'S POOR AN' YOUR BUTLER'S POOR

WE *ALSO* HAVE TO SUPPORT AN EXTREMELY POOR *CHAUFFEUR*

P6

THERE'S THE QUESTION OF RE-DISTRIBUTIN' YOUR GIFTS TO THE POOR— NAMELY *ME*

LISTEN POOR-GIRL YOU'RE WASTIN' YOUR TIME —I DI'N' *GET* ANY CHRIS'MAS PREZZIES

P7

CHRIS'MAS PREZZIES? NOT SO FAST THERE— *NOT* SO *FAST*

I WANT YOU TO *FIRST* OF ALL CAST YOUR MIND BACK TO YOUR *BIRTHDAY*— *OCTOBER* THE *TWENTY-FIFTH*

P.34

SOMETHIN'S GOIN' *ON* THERE, BOOT — I C'N *TELL*

P.35

MAISIE — ARE YOU RAVIN' (SPLUTTER) MAD?

YOU DELIBERATELY DROVE ME INTO THAT PIT OF FREEZIN' COLD WATER

BUT MARLON — TWAS FOR *LOVE*

STRANGE THINGS ARE DONE BY A WOMAN IN LOVE

OH YEA? — WOULD *YOU* JUMP INTO A PIT OF COLD WATER?

YES ♡

OH YES ♡

A THOUSAND TIMES — YES ♡

— IF IT WASN'T FOR THE FACT I MIGHT GET MY HAIR WET

P.36

P.37

P.40

MARLON— *LOOK OUT*

HE DID SAY SOMETHIN' ALWAYS HAPPENED TO HIM WHEN YOU WERE AROUN'

YOU'RE DOIN' THIS JUS' TO MAKE ME LOOK RIDICULOUS

P.41

WELL YOU'RE ALL RIGHT NOW KISSY-FACE

ALL'S WELL THAT ENDS WELL

ALL'S WELL WOT ENDS WELL ?

I'VE BEEN UP TO MY NECK IN A PIT OF FREEZIN' WATER

—FALLEN FROM THE CEILIN'

—RUN FULL-TILT INTO A BUS-STOP

AN' *YOU* SAY ALL'S WELL WOT ENDS WELL

CRUMBS MARLON — YOU DO GO ON

P.44

P.45

BOO

P.48

HEY— HOLD HARD THERE FELLOW

WHAT'S THAT RECENTLY ACQUIRED OBJECT YOU ARE HOLDING IN YOUR MOUTH?

OH—THIS ARE BEING A SIMILAR DEVICE TO THE ONE YOU WERE ISSUED

THE SECRET AGENT'S HEAVILY DISGUISED SMOKELESS CIGAR

WITH A *KNUCKLE JOINT* ON THE END?

...Mk. II

B.H.— THAT'S *MY* BONE YOU'VE GOT IN YOUR MOUTH

NO NO—I'M ASSURING YOU—IT'S A *DISGUISED CIGAR—ALL* US SECRET AGENTS HAVE THEM

P.49

HOW LONG HAVE *YOU* BEEN A SECRET AGENT?

—THAT'S A SECRET

—HOWEVER... YOU'VE NO DOUBT HEARD OF THE SPY WHO CAME IN FROM THE COLD?

YES

WELL HE WERE TAKING ME FOR A WALK AT THE TIME

P.54

P.55

P.58

P.59

SPRING IS SPRINGIN', BOOT. SPRING IS DEFINITELY SPRINGIN'

SAP IS SURGIN', BUDS ARE BULGIN' AN' UNDERNEATH OUR VERY FEET ROOTS ARE SQUIRMIN' ABOUT LIKE MAD

I THINK...

— HAVE A LOOK UNDER ONE O' THEM WRECKS AN' SEE IF ANYTHIN'S HAPPENIN'

IT'S ALL HAPPENIN' RIGHT ENOUGH — YOU C'N ALMOST FEEL IT BENEATH YOUR FEET

WOT?

SPRING — AN' NATURE AWAKENIN' AN' STUFF

I MEAN — RIGHT UNDER OUR VERY FEET

MILLIONS AN' BILLIONS OF ROOTS SEETHIN' ABOUT

TWISTIN' AN' TURNIN' AN' CREEPIN'

AN' SQUIRMIN' AN'...

HELP HELP ROOTS!

P. 66

P.67

P.70

P.71

The
Pied Piper
of Wormelin

THOSE WHO'VE MISSED THE LAST FEW EPISODES WILL BE COMPLETELY BAFFLED AS TO THE POINT OF THIS ONE — AND IT SERVES THEM RIGHT

THERE YOU ARE — OH 'GREAT LIBERATOR OF THE WORMS'

AN' *WHERE*, MAY ONE ASK ARE THE SQUIRMIN' LITTLE CHARMERS RIGHT NOW?

—resting

WHAT A GOOD IDEA — I THINK I'LL FOLLOW SUIT

AAAAHH

WELL trust *YOU* to go and wake them up again

BABY GRUMPLIN'— MUM SAID YOU WERE TO GET RID OF THOSE WORMS

HAVE YOU GOT RID OF THOSE WORMS ?

yes maisie

GAH

— i shan't be wanting any tea

BOOT—BOOT— BEN-THE-BUTCHER IN THE HIGH STREET IS OUT THERE GIVIN' AWAY TONS AN' TONS

OF SAUSAGES

HA-HA APRIL FOOL

....I THINK

P.78

P.79

MAISIE-FOR-MAY-QUEEN MAISIE-FOR-MAY-QUEEN MAISIE-FOR-MAY-QUEEN

LET'S HEAR IT FOR MAISIE

P.88

— I THINK I JUS' MET THE SILENT MAJORITY

HOW ABOUT *BRIBERY*, MARLON?

WOT?

— S'POSE I *BRIBED* YOU TO VOTE FOR ME TO BE MAY QUEEN?

WITH *ME*

I'M WILLIN' TO *SACRIFICE* MY *SWEET* YOUNG *SELF*

'MAGINE MY SOFT JUICE-EXTRACTIN' LIPS PRESSED AGAINST YOURS — MY WARM VIBRANT BODY YOURS TO...

COME BACK AN' BE CORRUPTED YOU PIG

P.89

I'M NOW ABOUT TO GIVE YOU AN ELECTION ADDRESS

9 SEABODY BUILDINGS, SETHNAL....

— SO MUCH FOR THE HUMOROUS APPROACH

P.96

WELL SINCE THE APPEAL TO *LOYALTY* DIN'T WORK AN' *BRIBERY* DIN'T WORK I'M GOIN' TO HAVE TO USE *REASON*

AN' THE *REASON* YOU'RE GOIN' TO VOTE FOR ME IS BERYL BOGEY — THE ALL-IN FREE-STYLE BLACK-BELT WOMAN'S LIBERATED NET-BALL CHAMPION, WHO'LL CLOBBER YOU IF YOU DON'T

URK URK URK

PSST — AN' THE SWEETIES — DON'T FORGET THE SWEETIES

OH YEA

AN' FOR THE SAME REASON YOU MIGHT CARE TO DONATE A LARGE BAG OF SWEETIES

THANKS PLAIN-JANE, I *KNEW* I WAS *RIGHT* TO INCLUDE AN *INTELLECTUAL* IN THE PARTY

P.97

P.98

P.99

HEY, MAISIE — HAVE YOU HEARD ABOUT MARLON INVENTIN' JOKES?

YES I *HAVE*, WELLIN'TON

HE'S INVITED *ME* AROUN' FOR A DEMONSTRATION OF HIS LATEST — THE 'INK-BLOT' JOKE

— WHICH HE HASN'T YET QUITE GOT THE HANG OF

P.106

'LO MARLON — GOT ANY MORE JOKES UP YOUR SLEEVE?

WAIT — I'LL TAKE A LOOK

— NO

BUT I *'AVE* INVENTED THE 'SNEEZIN' POWDER' JOKE

SNEEZIN' POWDER JOKE?

YEA — WOT 'APPENS IS THIS —

— I GET YOU TO STICK YOUR 'EAD IN THIS BIG BAG OF PEPPER ...

P.107

P.108

P.109

'ULLO SAILOR

BY THE LORD HARRY— IT'S TATTY OLDBITT —THE SAILORS' FRIEND

ARNCHA PLEESTA SEAMY?

GIVE US A KISS

MADAM— YOUR BREATH SMELLS OF *GIN*

WELL THERE'S A REASON FOR THAT (WHOOPS) DEARIE

— I CAN'T AFFORD TO DRINK CHANEL Nº 5

MADAM— *WOULD* YOU MIND RISING FROM THAT EXTREMELY UNDIGNIFIED *POSITION*

♪ ROLL ME OVER ROLL ME OVER ♪

WELL IT *DOES* HAVE A CERTAIN VULGAR TITILLATION WHICH IS WHY I'M ASKING YOU TO *DESIST*

UNDIGRIFIED? I THOUGHT IT WAS EXTREMELY PERVOCATIVE

ARE YOU ASKING ME TO FORGET I'M A GENTLEMAN?

OH COME ON DEARIE — GIVE A GIRL A GRAPPLE

NO, RUG-FACE, JUST ASKIN' YOU TO REMEMBER YOU'RE ALSO A DIRTY OLE DOG

P. 118

P. 119

CUTE LI'L BUNDLES OF FLUFF THEY MAY BE — BUT THOSE DUCKS'RE GOIN' TO HAVE TO **GO**

QUACK

P.132

FOR ONE THING — WHAT'RE THEY GOIN' TO **EAT** ? — THERE'S NOTHIN' **HERE** FOR THEM TO EAT

THIS IS **QUACKMAIL**

QUACK QUACK QUACK
QUACK
QUACK QUACK
QUACK

RIGHT YOU LOT — I'VE MANAGED TO SCRATCH TOGETHER A BIT OF A MEAL FOR YOU

BUT AFTER THIS Y'GOTTA **GO**

QUACK QUACK

QUACK QUACK QUACK

BITSA BROKEN BISCUITS — CHOC'LATE CAKE — DUNDEE — THE REMNANTS OF MAISIE'S BIRTHDAY CAKE...

IF DUCKS LIVED LIKE THIS ALL THE TIME...

QUACK QUACK QUACK QUARF

P.133

QUARF ARF ARF

KNOCK IT OFF, BOOT

QUACK QUACK
QUACK QUACK QUACK

P.142

P.143

P.146

P.147

TAKE YOUR PLACES FOR THE SACK RACE

P.152

SACK NUMBER TWO REPORT TO THE JUDGES' TABLE

MARLON'S LININ' UP FOR THE HIGH JUMP

YOO-HOO MARL... OH I *DON'T BELIEVE* IT

WELL — THERE'S A *SORT* OF SENSE TO IT

P.153

P.154

P.155

COMMENCING THE FINALS FOR THE POLE-VAULT

CONTESTANTS ONE

TWO

AND THREE REPORT TO THE JUDGES' TABLE

P.156

THE MARATHON'S COMIN' IN

DIRTY McSQUIRTY'S WAY OUT IN FRONT

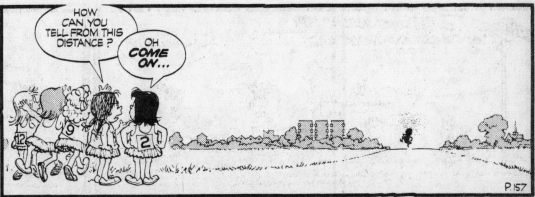

HOW CAN YOU TELL FROM THIS DISTANCE?

OH COME ON...

P.157

P.158

P.159

P.164

P.165

YOU D'LIBERATELY TOOK A CHANCE ON ME BEIN' POISONED

P.168

YOU PIG, YOU MORON, YOU SHUFFLE-FOOTED...

GROIN-FACED SEWER-BRAINED SELFISH...

BONK

OH WELL—IF I CAN'T JUS' 'AVE A CIVILISED FRIEN'LY DISCUSSION

GRONE

FIRS' YOU TRY TO POISON ME AN' THEN YOU 'IT ME WHEN I WASN' LOOKIN'—I SHOULDA LISSENED TO MOTHER SHE WARNED ME I ...

A BONE!

WOT?

IT'S A BONE—A GINORMOUS BONE—COR! I'LL BET THERE'S 'UNDREDS O'BITS OF MICROSCOPIC MEAT CLINGIN' TO IT!

DON' BE RIDICULOUS

WOT?

LOOKA TH' *SIZE* OF IT—WOT KINDER ANIMAL WOULD'VE BONES *THAT* SIZE? IT'D COLLAPSE UNDER ITS OWN WEIGHT—IT'S A BIOLOGIGOGGLE IMPOSSIBILITY

REELY?

DID YOU KNOW THAT BILE O'LOGIGOGGLE PUSSY-BILLY-TEES 'AS 'UNDREDS O'BITS OF MICROSCOPIC MEAT CLINGIN' TO'EM *(CHEW CHEW)*

I WAS JUS' GETTIN' 'ROUN' TO THAT—IT'S A WELL-KNOWN FAC' *(CHEW NIBBLE CHEW)*

P.169

P.172

P.173

P. 176

P.177

P.188

P.189

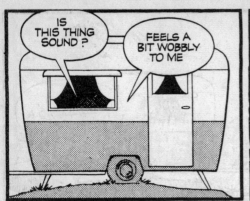

P.200

P.201

P.240

P.241

P.254

P.255

P.260

P.261

P.262

P.263